Winter Ride

By Carolyn j Morris

wheeee
cjmorris

Illustrated by Richard McNaughton

www.railfencebooks.com

Printed in Canada

ISBN 978-0-9876821-5-4

PRO121 08 2015

Winter Ride

Chick and Duckling went out one day,
through the snow on a little, red sleigh.

zip, zip, slip, slip

slide, slide, glide, glide

wheeeeeeeeeeeeeee

Past the tractor, past the plough,
too late in the season to harvest now!

zip, zip, slip, slip

slide, slide, glide, glide

wheeeeeeeeeeeeeeee

Beside the bucket, beside the pump,
water is frozen, watch out for the bump!

zip, zip, slip, slip

slide, slide, glide, glide

wheeeeeeeeeeeeeee

Through the yard, through the gate,
we're on our way, no time to wait!

zip, zip, slip, slip

slide, slide, glide, glide

wheeeeeeeeeeeeeee

Bunch

Across the field, across the snow,
this is fun, but a little slow!

zip, zip, slip, slip

slide, slide, glide, glide

wheeeeeeeeeeeeeeee

Down the hill, down they go,
very fast, so stay down low!

zip, zip, slip, slip

slide, slide, glide, glide

wheeeeeeeeeeeeeee

Over the pond, over the ice,
slipping and sliding is rather nice!

zip, zip, slip, slip

slide, slide, glide, glide

wheeeeeeeeeeeeeee

Into the woods, into the trees,
it's calm here, away from the breeze!

zip, zip, slip, slip

slide, slide, glide, glide

wheeeeeeeeeeeeeeee

Under the branches, under the boughs,
a little tired with no time to drowse!

zip, zip, slip, slip

slide, slide, glide, glide

wheeeeeeeeeeeeeee

Let's go Chick and Duckling.
Back through the snow, crunch, crunch.
Time to join the Railfence Bunch.

zip, zip, slip, slip

slide, slide, glide, glide

wheeeeeeeeeeeeeee

zip, zip, slip, slip

slide, slide, glide, glide

wheeeeeeeeeeeeee

About the Author

Carolyn's country roots began on the family farm on the 10th line of the old Nottawasaga Township. Carolyn j Morris has taught in both Toronto and rural communities for 30 years, and each spring she shares baby chicks and ducklings with her Junior Kindergarten students and in the communities around her home and school.
www.railfencebooks.com

About the Illustrator

Richard McNaughton is an award-winning artist whose works are hanging in private collections throughout North America and Europe. Working in both watercolour and acrylic, Richard's art reflects his love for the rural countryside, especially the Grey/Bruce area of Ontario, where he has lived for 28 years.
richardmcnaughton.wordpress.com